THE OWL AND THE PUSSYCAT

AND OTHER POEMS

This edition published in 2009
The Dedalus Press
13 Moyclare Road
Baldoyle
Dublin 13
Ireland

www.dedaluspress.com

ISBN 978 1 906614 19 5

Dedalus Press titles are represented in North America by Syracuse University Press, Inc., 621 Skytop Road, Suite 110, Syracuse, New York 13244, and in the UK by Central Books, 99 Wallis Road, London E9 5LN

The Dedalus Press receives financial assistance from The Arts Council / An Chomhairle Ealaíon

THE OWL AND THE PUSSYCAT

AND OTHER POEMS

Tom Mathews

DEDALUS PRESS
DUBLIN, IRELAND

ACKNOWLEDGEMENTS

Acknowledgements are due to the editors of the following in which a number of these poems originally appeared:

Poetry Ireland Review, Cúirt Annual, Crannog, The Stony Thursday Book, In Dublin and *Force 10.*

Barbara Streisand: "Sometimes I feel like an insect."
George Segal: "Kafka."
Barbara Streisand: "Yeah. That's it. A kafka."

—*The Owl and the Pussycat* (1970)

In Memoriam Benedict Kiely

You were a shell at the end
But I heard the sea.

Contents

THE OWL AND THE PUSSYCAT

AND OTHER POEMS

In the National Gallery

Sue Ellen slips her Docs off,
Dad surfs the new DeLillo,
Mom asks the torpid guard: 'Is this
The way to a Murillo?'

The winter sunlight blazes,
The dustmotes dance in air,
Through cracked brown Windsor glazes
The painted heroes stare.

Simplex

Crossword puzzle girl at bar—
Four letters (heavenly body). 'Star', I said.
She said, 'You are,'

And took my pen and filled it in.
'Drink,' I said. 'Three letters, Gin?'
'I will,' she said.

Problem her. Solution me.
'Do you take this man to be?'
'I do,' she said.

Girl on Mobile

Hi. I got this phone for my birthday.
—Gift
Guess what was on the National Geographic channel last night.
Some small white-spotted fish like turbot…
—Brill.
…And a polar bear.
—Cool.
And a poisonous snake
—Deadly.
Then I watched a programme about Venus Williams.
—Ace.
And a documentary about Heroin.
—Gear

We *must* do something about that girl's vocabulary.

Aquarelle

Flowers in a looking glass
She breathes upon. Their dying shades
That grade and meld will waste and pass.
The patient fanblades' dusty lathes
Turn light, and dark, and all banal
As snow, as charcoal, as her hair,
As dogmerds by the dull canal
When the white swans are nesting there.

Once was a child with child's delight,
Sunlight was big and starlight small.
Dreams of her morning fade at night
Moving in carlights on the wall.
Chiaroscuro days that were
Soft lit by Dodgson or Daguerre.

Parnassus

When we ascend Parnassus one of the days
How shall we go?
In Johnson's futurity referenceless post-chaise
Or Beckett's deux chevaux?

Have talk with Jarry and Queneau of paronomasia
And dine alfresco with napkins on our knees
And listen to Joyce murder 'The Jewel of Asia.'
And T.S. Eliot complaining about the cheese?

And witness the motionless dance of Ribemont Dessaignes
While Henry James reads from *Harper's Bazaar*
Till we fall asleep to the all but audible strains
Of Edith Sitwell playing the air guitar?

Visiting the Locked Ward

Lights waltz like petals in her waterjug,
Watching which random choreography
She says, 'They talk about me. Later on
The birds will corkscrew out of the night like that.'

Penguin Beckett, packet of sanitary towels
Caught in the pulsing violet ambulance light.
'Love,' she says, 'is a mouse in a forest of owls
And I burn in the morning before I am delivered.'

And I burn in the morning.

More Daffodils

One in a rusting barrow in Knockdoe,
Bright among brown sods.

One clutched in the hand of the concrete Christ
In the rain at John of God's.

Flashback

Woman delights her not, nor man
This idle evening. Lillian,
Video in fast rewind mode,
Watches the blood-dark buds implode.

Like rubies ranked at Tiffany's
Or blows up pixels with the mouse
Dreaming of the epiphany
That happened in the lion house.

At Dublin Zoo, two winters past,
When the white tiger spoke to her
Until her heart pumped blood so fast
That everything became a blur

Of lights and sound. Rewind. Reload.
Watch as the blood-red buds implode.

Seabirds in the Inner Cities

Seabirds in the inner cities
Stain the statues on their plinths
And the minotaur is howling
Blinded in the labyrinth.

In the Trojan Horse a soldier,
Swearing, eases out a splinter.
Snowflakes fill the Yeti's footprint
Somewhere in the dead of winter.

Prostrate now, the native mages
Venerate the great gorilla.
Weeping women watch the smoke
Ascending from the torched flotilla.

Miles away the narwhal glides
Through the circumpolar tides.

Lux Mundi

Mary dreamed Frankenstein from disparate parts,
One of them Byron's size.
Shelley thought eyes her nipples in a dream
That Polidori could not analyse.

Afloat, asleep in amniotic waves
George Gordon needs no orthopaedic boot.
Dreaming of days at Cambridge with his bear:
Which was creation's Lord, and which was brute?

The great insomniac who dreams them all,
Whose contemplation fixes stars and suns,
Smiles on his son who gave the world Don Juan
As on a convent full of sleeping nuns,

Looks in the heart of the old shabby bear
And sends him dreams of marzipan and buns.

The Ballad of Jeems Joker

I will dwell in Trieste
With me eyes full of Rheum.
Too old to play Stephen
Too cold to play Bloom.

Too exhausted to bother
With credence or doubt
I'll play upon words
Till the light is gone out.

Goodbye now, goodbye. Annalyse all I said.
Remember how genius arose from 'The Dead'.
What's forged in the spirit remains to the eye
And history's cyclic, goodbye now goodbye.

Proteus

'Close your eyes and see, Monsieur Jolas,'
Said Joyce, post operative. The muted light
Soft on the bandaged eyes. C'est vrai hélas
Que Milton dit, 'And day brought back my night.'

My rainbows flicker out? Mais c'est la vie.
Ça va, on aperçoit malgré les yeux.
J'ai lu les écritures de la nuit.
'Lettres et le néon,' calembour affreux.

Blind drunk, or blind, night comes that has no pity.
A plague upon it.
From nights of words I wrought a brazen city
Of glimmering Allstars, Mornstar, Lunestare, Comet.

Silver Wig

Tripping under anaesthetic
In Blahnik heels he hosts affairs
Where witty picaninnies picnic
With Theda Bara teddy bears.

Mapplethorpe horned and tumescent
Watches the strobelights blind the squares,
While, dressed in something iridescent,
Valerie, alone upstairs,

Reviews her violent memories, slowly
Sighs as the cellbars' shades go brown,
Turns up 'The Houses of the Holy'
And turns the dimmer switches down.

Elsewhere the surgeon and the staff
Saw Andy Warhol's chest in half.

Goya

The grave self-painted eyes are dark as pitch.
Behold the Maja naked, and the bitch
Black as the vestments when they burn a witch
In dumbshow on the wall of his apartment.

The birthday cake Infanta dead at six,
The madmen's eyes turned down to smoking wicks
Red as the ochre lichen on the bricks—
The inquisition's dirty tricks department.

The bloody child at staring Saturn's maw,
The torsos in the bare trees. 'This I saw.'
All human nature red in tooth and claw
His contemplation.

To rail at man's misdeeds was all his art.
Now mixing black with black he stands to start
The crucifixion that can move the heart
To more than contemplation.

Villon

I'd like to warm my hands on some old flame,
Rake up the ashes till they're red again
To recommence the old lugubrious game.
The lighted ferries drift along the Seine.

Now, when the shadows of the autumn leaves
In rue St. Victoire move on the yellow wall,
I thrust my freezing fists into my sleeves.
The parish priest whistles the march from *Saul.*

Ice in the gutters cracks beneath my feet.
There's chicken gravy on the Reverend's chin.
My shirt is colder than a winding sheet.
My sheepskin coat fetched fifty sous for gin.

He gives his blessing, for a blessing's free.
No wounds of nails are in his well-heeled palms.
I'll rest my back against this dying tree
And starve before I'll ask the cunt for alms.

Two Dreams of Painters

I

Picasso at a café table
Buys roses,
Throws the flowers away,
Flattens the wrapper,
And draws a carnival of animals.

II

Max Ernst knocks at the gate of heaven.
Jesus, disguised as Loplop, lets him in.

Asses' Milk

The sun that melts the snowman in the yard
Glads my grim heart.
And I am glad to see the man of snow
Turn in his death to water that is life.

The ruby of the merlot in the glass
Joys my rubbed nose
And when it flowers in fire along the vein
Will turn again to water at the end.

The nib now mimicking the beaks of larks
Jets my white page.
And I am stunned to see the sentence form
Unbidden as the shadow of my beard.

The sun that warms the scarecrow in the field
Gilds my grey soul
Till I am moved to dance upon my grave
Shifting its gravel with my slippered feet.

Housmanesque

The snow that bends the branches
Will melt. And stars will die.
In meads the moonlight blanches,
The fallen legions lie.

And so will you and I.

Clockface

I am the Minister for Agriculture and Fisheries.
I've a pig in the bubblecar.
I fish for compliments with a bent pin
And I plant my seeds by moonlight with my wife
Who is a harpist in Bunratty Castle.
She plays behind a curtain
Because she has a harelip.
When she plays for me I dance in luminous boots
On the *Farming Independent,*
And I smack a big heap of peat briquettes
With a jam roll.
But the best crack yet
Was the time I hopped backwards around Ireland
On one leg.

Gogarty Watches Yeats Give his Son a Piggyback Ride

On the poet's shoulder high
He laughs to see the world go by.
Reversed is old Caligula's course:
The senator's become the horse.

4WH

The game will last till later
The pirate flag is furled
Tall nanny is dictator
Of all the nursery world.

Death is a man with a sickle
Love is a babe at the breast
And time ticks away to a trickle
When Nanny lays down to rest.

The radio stutters static
The locks rust in the doors
And dust piles deep in the attic
Of the Home and Colonial Stores.

Here Come the James Fentonettes

There's a bluff chap with a sixpack
There's a svelte bitch in a triptych
There's a blind date at a checkpoint
And a cheap trick with a lipstick

So spike that scotch
Praise that past
Patch that scratch
With elastoplast

There's an ash blonde at the cashpoint
There's an axed trunk in the driveway
There's a sick drunk at a flashpoint
And a spent match in the ashtray

So mute that mike
Shoot that shite
Off that dyke
With an armalite

There's a bitch with an arse for a brainpan
There's a kook with his dick in a cupcake
And his babe's in the wood
Singing 'Johnny B. Goode'
Cause she isn't too quick on the uptake.

News from the Old Country

When every line was a crossed line
Every piece was a show piece
Every cross was a Shawcross
And every McNiece was an Apple McNiece

Every edition was a first edition
Every age was a coming of age
Every act was an act of contrition
Every cage was a gilded cage.

2

Every cage was a gilded cage
Every Shaw was a kickshaw
Everyman was a Zimmerman
And every Ricks his rickshaw

Every bear was a Pooh Bear
Every bah was a big poobah
Every frock was a Prufrock
And every pére was Ubu Pére.

3

When every pére was Ubu Pére
Lou and Andy sang *Andalucia*
Every Dylan was a Thomas Mann
And every Fonze a fons bandusiae

When every whore was a write hoor
Every Lane was a Dialstone
Every heure was a Flann heure
And every Myles was a milestone.

4

When every Myles was a milestone
Every hack drove the barman barmy
Every soldier was a dead soldier
Every army was a standing army.

Every cough was a coffin nail
Every drink was a *deoch an doras*
Every feed was a feed of ale
Every chorus was a croaking chorus.

5

Every chorus was a croaking chorus
Every bede had his bidet
Every see was a Sargasso Sea
And every deed had its D-day.

Every D-day was an LSD day
Every sou was an aperçu
Every dime was a paradigm
And every quid a 'Quid Rides?'

6

When every quid is a 'Quid Rides?'
Every line is a line in the sand
Every but is a buttress
And every and is an ampersand.

Every rhyme is a half rhyme
Every verse is too clever by half
When fool's gold maketh the golden calf
Every line is a crossed line.

How Sumo

How does sumo
Become sensitive writer of haiku?
Li Po suction.

Young Men in Spats

—You look like Bertie Wooster with that hoe.
—What hoe?
—Now you're talking like Bertie Wooster.

'As New York Raged Round Me'

As New York raged round me
(It's my kind of town)
I took out my laptop
And had a sit down

And as folk of all nations
Flowed about me and ebbed
By Grand Central Station
I sat down and webbed.

'One Night I'

One night I ended up in a flat in Rathmines
With a girl who told me she used to go out
With Paul Hewson. I sat on the bed and read
Her Beckett's verse:

It's rather fun, though not such fun as sex,
Reciting *Echo's Bones* to Bono's ex.

Little Richard

Beating the keys of the great white Steinway,
Screaming the songs in the smoky room,
Crouched on the lid like a Fuseli homunculus:
AWOPBOPALOOBOPALOPBAMBOOM.

In Memoriam Anthony Burgess

Joydrunk behind your wall of fire
You grubbed while all were lazing,
Vamped Formby riffs on Homer's lyre
And went down all guns blazing.

Gogo's Song

A tree. The wind. A moon. Ho hum.
Don't suppose Godot's going to come.

Sinus Headache

Does the initial sentence draw you in?
Or this one keep you reading till the next?
Which this one is. Will you, most hope abandoned,
Elicit something from the vexing text?

The fifth, I think (and that's a quarter score),
Has even less of piquancy or zest
Than that dry version it replaces here,
Rendering deadlier dull the palimpsest.

The ninth (the muses' number and this line's),
Two added to seven (number of days in week),
Completes (almost) a verse entirely wanting
In subject matter, meaning and technique.

The couplet, luckless reader, now appears
Which like the verse should bore you all to tears.

What the Sirens Sang

Hard questions asked
In other times and lands:
Pilate said, 'What is truth?'
And washed his hands.

'Half empty, or half full?'
Enquired an ass.
Socrates took a pull
And drained the glass.

'Who fished the murex up?
What porridge had John Keats?'
Porridge of dark arterial blood
And rubies on the reeking sheets.

Astronomy

New star in the Plough
Tonight. Comet-quick. Ice-bright.
Concorde's red tail-light.

Camden St.

In Sunday's phone booth
A silver box:
Last night's sweet and sour.

Last Bus

Watching a drunken girl sleep past her stop
Clutching the final straw—
Berry Alcopop.

Madman. Twilight. Portobello Bridge

He rests.
He's had a busy afternoon.
Sixteen swans to say hello to.
And the man in the moon.

Self at 53

Cast off. Set sail now for some new-found land.
Explain. (Your wife could never understand.)
Take Yeat's 'After Ronsard' from the shelf.
Trot out the tried and tested old routines.
Tell one last younger woman what life means
Before you find out what life meant yourself.

'Rain falls like night'

Rain falls like night on Londonderry
Where, although couples do make merry,
Those of the Catholic communion
Tend to avoid the act of union.

Craig Raine Says

Craig Raine says you've got to get their attention
In fifty words.

Come on, you bastards—Only twenty-eight to go…

Channel-Zapping

The blind man learns the candle flame has form.
Sharp-hooved giraffes can disembowel a lion.
Neanderthals buried their dead in flowers.
Beethoven said, 'I shall hear my work in heaven.'

Cut-Up Poem

Yeats / Daily Sport *Phone Sex ads, Tuesday 11.05.93*

Never give all the heart for love
RUB IT SHOOT IT ALL IN JUST "TWO MINUTES"
Will hardly seem worth thinking of
BORED LONELY WIVES WANT SEXY DAYTIME FUN
To passionate women if it seem
JACKIE MAKES SEX NOISES ON THE PHONE
Certain, and they never dream
MASKED LEATHER GIRLS TEASE THEN CHAIN YOU UP
That it fades out from kiss to kiss
LETS TOUCH TONGUES AND LICK
For everything that's lovely is
SMOOTH BUM, BLACK DIRTY STOCKINGS
But a brief dreamy kind delight
TEN SECOND JERK OFF 0338418928
O never give the heart outright
GET IT OUT AND PLAY WITH IT (I AM)
For they for all smooth lips can say
I'LL BEND OVER AND RUB MYSELF AGAINST THE PHONE
Have given their hearts up to the play
I'LL BE YOUR SEX PLAYMATE. ENJOY ME FULLY.
And who could play it well enough
TWO GIRLS WITH SALTY MOUTHS
If deaf and dumb and blind with love ?
LICK MY TOES THROUGH NYLON HOSE
He that made this knows all the cost
36p MIN CHEAP RATE 48p MIN ALL OTHER TIMES
For he gave all his heart and lost.

Mengele

He sees them sweep the leaves in piles,
Remembers Auschwitz. And he smiles.

Lapid Opera

Three syllables trip off the tongue
The moving pen with life investing
A Balthus nymph forever young,
Beyond the pale, and interesting.

The six-day moon, car window held,
Where, under real and spectral crescents,
Words like fritillaries impaled
Are headlit blurs of iridescence,

And, by a subtle synthesis,
Fuse in the little clockwork heart
Coppelia's dance, Galatea's kiss
And Fragonard's with Beardsley's art,

And gun the engine of desire.
Hum, Lo, sweet chariot of fire.

Love Again

I've been through all that shit before.
Please, Sir, can I have some more?

After McGough

You opened the door in my heart
With the catch in your throat.

False Start

I and Pangur Bán my dog.

The Owl and the Pussycat

Henry James had two kings names.
But so I fear did Edward Lear.

Inishbofin

In the windbent grass I'll want no clock.
Chonas ata tú? crows the cock
To nettlecaught wool and rainwet rock.

Wet wharf, wet nets, wet ropes, wet crates,
Wet ferns, wet sands, wet hay, wet gates,
Wet birds, wet sheep, wet cows, wet slates,
Wet drunks from the United States—

On Bofin.

In Memoriam Michael Hartnett

When we drank
He sometimes asked for a cartoon
For his partner
If he was late
Or one over the eight.

Months after he died,
Opening her bag she asked, 'Remember these?'
Bar doodles: fish, rhinoceri, a dog with wings.
A child's purse full of useless things.

Song

Sang the giddy blood
In the gold sun,
'Every hour is good
Till the world's done.'

Sang ice in a pool
And the north wind,
'Though the world is cruel
Never be unkind.'

'O where is love?'
Sang a little rose,
And a dim star answered
'Nobody knows.'

'And what has set
Your heart alight?'
Sang the soft owl
In the dark night.

O the sea sang true
As I walked alone,
'One is half of two,
Two are half of one.'

The Green Hill

The lovers, sated, are asleep at length
Where the sprung trap has spent its tensile strength
Snapping the brown rat's spine, dousing with blood
The white slow piling ashes. The new wood

Splits in the oven, hisses and subsides.
The dreamers murmur like the moonpulled tides.
The wind brings salt from breakers blue and cold
Up the green hill. Above, the aeroplanes

Bear winking rubies through the black and gold,
And, candle-blinded at the window panes,
The soft moths flutter from the sooty beams.
The sleepers drifting in their differing dreams

Safe in the smokescreen of the sputtering turf
Are seabright spindrift in the shifting surf.

Theorem

Is sex the answer? Or is love
A theorem anyone can prove?
Is this new beating of our hearts
More than the sum of our private parts?

Just Williams

This is just to say
That I have left William Carlos William's poems
In the ice box.
Forgive me.
They were so sweet.
But so cold.

The Heart

The heart of the adult human male is the size of two clenched fists

The heart's the size
Of two clenched fists.
I planted a garden
In autumn mists.

I thinned out seed,
You hung out clothes.
I knelt to weed
About the rose.

The flowers grew,
We grew apart.
And I turned my green-thumbed fists
Back to a human heart.

'John Ruskin dreamed'

John Ruskin dreamed a delicate spiral tower
Millais had sketched for him in pink and white
Aberdeen granite ringlets. Rose's bower
Had shocked into his consciousness one night.

Then lightning for an instant saw him climb
The witches' staircase of the boiling sheets.
The tower sucked down by all-devouring time
A sugar stick a hairless Gretel eats.

It felt as if he'd seen a ship go down
Behind a Turner sun, its sails aflame.
He, the tall captain, knowing he must drown,
Stood fast. And then the final darkness came.

Alexandria

As tigers pacing in a winter zoo
For what they know not under alien stars
Pad silently behind the shadow bars,
Remembering the moon in the bamboo,

So Borges in a silent library
Pauses alone upon a midnight stair
Hunting by moonlight, when no moon is there
A sort of tiger no one else can see.

Xerox

Paper under glass.
A snow field. A lightning flash.
Two poems now at last.

Elba

Watching the whales spout,
Napoleon remembers
Fountains at Versailles.

En Route

Some travel light aboard the Honours bus,
Bursting with promise into a promised land.
I shiver, waiting with the rest of us
Here for the Pass bus, bus pass in my hand.

Homeopath

You can heal the heart, you say,
But you can not—
Since seeing you so little
Makes me want to such a lot.

Charity

With her new love
My old drives past.
Oh flag lady, fly your flags
At half mast.

Tomorrow

"Sit down and I'll get us a couple of beers,
Here, borrow my hanky and dry your tears,
It'll all be the same in a hundred years
And things will be better tomorrow, my darling,
Things will be better tomorrow.

For the world each day is minted new,
And the sun is gold and the sky is blue,
And if that's a lie it's a good lie too
And things will be better tomorrow, my darling,
Things will be better tomorrow."

O silver the river and yellow the sand
And fair as a flower from a faraway land
Is the girl with her hand in his faithless hand.

The Dark

The dark? My darling, after fifty-two
You find the light is good for whistling too.

Dedalus Press

Poetry from Ireland and the world

Established in 1985, the Dedalus Press is one of Ireland's best-known literary imprints, dedicated to new Irish poetry and to poetry from around the world in English translation.

For further information on Dedalus Press titles, or to access our Audio Room of free-to-download recordings by many of the writers on our list, visit

www.dedaluspress.com

Lightning Source UK Ltd.
Milton Keynes UK
11 January 2011

165514UK00001B/11/P